WILDSCAPE

WILDSCAPE

Kenneth Steven

Tu best wishes,

Ken

PETERLOO POETS

First published in 2007
by Peterloo Poets
The Old Chapel, Sand Lane, Calstock,
Cornwall PL18 9QX, U.K.

**A catalogue record for this book is available
from the British Library**

ISBN 9781904324485

Printed in Great Britain
By 4word Ltd, Unit15, Baker's Park, Bristol BS13 7TT

ACKNOWLEDGEMENTS

Poems in Wildscape have appeared in the following literary outlets:

The Writer (US), The London Magazine, Poetry Review, The Sydney Morning Herald (Australia), Westerly (Australia), The Scots Magazine, Haiku Quarterly, Abraxas, New Writing Scotland, Hollin's Critic (US), Staple, The Countryman, The Herald (Glasgow), Envoi, Salt (Australia), Scintilla, The Antigonish Review (Canada), Planet, Chapman, Pulsar, Markings and Northwords Now

Several poems in the collection have been broadcast on BBC Radio 4.

Supported by
The National Lottery®
through Arts Council England

This collection is dedicated to Roger Sylvester, my first teacher

CONTENTS

The Last Wolf

The last wolf in Scotland is not dead
Only sleeping.

He is no shaggy dog story
In the corries and crags of Cairngorm.

He is never in danger of being killed,
But rather dying of neglect.

If the last wolf promised to renounce violence
He would be allowed to lie by any peat fire in Scotland.

But his paws keep the memories of battles
And there is smoke in the grey of his eyes.

He has waited here two hundred years and more
For a blizzard that might flay the summer

From our soft hands and old excuses.

Island

I remember what it was like to barefoot that house,
Wood rooms bleached by light. Days were new voyages,
                                              journeys,
Coming home a pouring out of stories and of starfish.
The sun never died completely in the night,
The skies just turned luminous, the wind
Tugged at the strings in the grass like a hand
In a harp. I did not sleep, too glad to listen by a window
To the sorrow sounds of the birds
As they swept down in skeins, and rose again, celebrating
All that was summer. I did not sleep, the weight of school
Behind and before too great to waste a grain of this.
One four in the morning at first larksong I went west over
                                              the dunes,
Broke down running onto three miles of white shell sand,
                                              and stood.
A wave curled and silked the shore in a single seamless
                                              breath.
I went naked into the water, ran deep into a green
Through which I was translucent. I rejoiced
In something I could not name; I celebrated a wonder
Too huge to hold. I trailed home, slow and golden,
Dried by the sunlight.

The Birth of the Foal

My eyes still fought with sleep. Out over the fields
Mist lay in grey folds, from vague somewheres
Curlews rose up with thin trails of crying. Our lanterns
Rocked in soft globes of yellow, our feet
Slushed through the early morning thickness of the grass.

She lay on her side, exhausted by her long night;
The hot smell of flanks and head and breath
Ghosted from her spread length.
Sunlight cracked from the broken yolk of the skies,
Ruptured the hills, spangled our eyes and blinded us,
Flooded the pale glows of our lanterns.

There he lay in a pool of his own wetness:
Four long spindles scrabbling, the bigness of his head, a bag
                                                    of a body –
All struggling to find one another, to join up, to glue
Into the single flow of a birthright. He fought
For the first air of his life, noised like a child.

His mother, still raw and torn from the scar of his birth,
Turned, and her eyes held him,
The great harsh softness of her tongue stilled his struggle.

We knelt in the wet grass, dumbed
By a miracle, by something bigger than the sun.

The Well

I found a well once
In the dark green heart of a wood

Where pigeons ruffled up into a skylight of branches
And disappeared.

The well was old, so mossed and broken
It was almost a part of the wood

Gone back to nature. Carefully, almost fearfully,
I looked down into its depths

And saw the lip of water shifting and tilting,
Heard the music of dripping stones.

I stretched down, cupped a deep handful
Out of the winter darkness of its world

And drank. That water tasted of moss, of secrets,
Of ancient meetings, of laughter,

Of dark stone, of crystal –
It reached the roots of my being

Assuaged a whole summer of thirst.
I have been wandering for that water ever since.

Daffodils

They flurry over the first raw green of the hills,
Trumpet the Easter fields;
Bright flags with their orange yolks
Bending under the flaying cruelty of April winds.

As if to prove that Calvin got it wrong,
That dark-lipped Luther in the cold austerity of history
Threw away the warm laughter of love
For the bare bones of theology.

The Kingfisher

One early May we went there, on foot,
Through the ghostly cobwebs of the morning,
Hearing the curlews rising in hauntings across the fields.
The land was muddy, a guttural rushing of syllables
After long spring rain, so our boots were sucked and glutted
By a swilling of mire. We struggled through screens of
                                                    trees,
Nets of rain meshing our faces, till we broke out
By that little trickle of stream –
Nothing more than a slither of thick water
Rippling away in different shades of inks.

Then, from nowhere, that blue bolt came
Bright as a dragonfly, a bit of summer sky,
Low as some skiffed stone, threading the reeds
To catch a branch, to lock
Into the sapphire thrill of kingfisher.
We stood amazed, gazing, ages,
Unable to believe the piece of luck we'd stumbled on.
We have kept that blue ever since
Somewhere in the winter attics of our world –
A priceless place, a whole kingdom.

The Small Giant

The otter is ninety percent water
Ten percent God.

This is a mastery
We have not fathomed in a million years.

I saw one once, off the teeth of western Scotland,
Playing games with the Atlantic –

Three feet of gymnastics
Taking on an ocean.

Geese

This morning I caught them
Against the headlands of rain
Glowering in from the west;
Half a hundred twinklings
In the angry sky, a gust of somethings
Grey against the greyness.

And then they turned in one gust
To climb the April sky
North, become a sprinkling of snowflakes
Underlit, to rise into a single skein –
An arrowhead ploughing the wind.

And I knew them as geese and stood watching
Their homing for Iceland;
I stood in the first splinters of rain
Watching until they were gone
And with them all my winter.

The Strangest Gift

Sister Mary Teresa gave me a wasp's nest from the convent
                                                   garden –
Just the startings, the first leaves, a cocoon of whisperings –
Made out of thousands of buzzings.
To think that these yellow-black thugs
Could make such finery, such parchment,
A whole home telling the story of their days,
Written and wrought so perfect
Stung me, remembering how I'd thumped them
With thick books, reduced them to squashes on walls,
Nothing more than broken bits on carpets.
This little bowl, this bit of beginning
Rooted out by the gardener, reminds me
Of something bigger I keep choosing to forget,
About what beauty is, and where that beauty's found.

A Day in April

Twelve o'clock. She stands in the back porch,
Strands of gold hair tangling her face.
She calls his name; her voice is blown away.
He looks up nonetheless, as though he's heard
Somewhere deep inside. Light scours the hills,
Gullies of wind sweep back the shadow.
Fleet's heard her, flows down the field
In a bouncing waterfall of black and white.
She smiles. A lamb pities the air
With a cry as thin as milk. She turns inside.

He thuds the mud from his boots.
Has the mail come? Delivery from Hulberts?
The clock flickers softly in the hall;
Up in the landing window the blue of April
A rippling flag of sky –
This land is in his hands
As surely as it ran his father's.
At the table she rumbles the potatoes from the pan,
Looks at him with soft eyes. I've good news, she murmurs.

Voices

The woodpecker taps out Morse,
Crows scrawl arguing across dawn in German.

Woodpigeons make soft French love words
As little twigs of sparrows chatter in Italian.

The raven is Norse, his voice chipped from sharp cliffs,
And geese squabble over Icelandic sagas.

In the middle of winter all I hear are the curlews,
Crying at night their Gaelic laments.

Saturdays

We used to go there for eggs –
A farm track with that green vein
Sprouting the middle rut. The farm crouched
Like some aggressive wildcat on the ground
Whose yellow eyes were windows. The whole yard strutted
And bagpiped with chickens. I always feared the dogs –
Two streamlined waterfalls of black and white,
Tongues like hot bacon, their barks
Gunning my heart with fear. But the farmer's wife
Brought us inside to the kitchen's hum,
The scent of mown hay green in the room.
We talked about foxes and new roads and prices,
My lips burned on hot tea. The eggs were still warm,
Dunged and tickled with straw.
We squeaked them in sixes into boxes,
Went out across the yard as a blue sky
Switched with swallows, waved to her wide smile
On the long bounce home.

The Frogs

The hills were low and furry;
We curved the hill road, into the warm dark,
Saying things in snatches, wrapped in night wool.
Out of our headlights the frozen ghost of an owl
Was gone.

We saw the frogs gradually –
They grew into shadows out of the road's soft stone.
We slowed to a hum, leaned forwards to watch them;
They were luminous and rubbery,
Some with one webbed hand raised, but all listening:
Heads held erect, hearing some ancient song,
Something that had called them into this strange river
In the sudden jolt of spring.

We edged the car round them, slow as a cyclist
Might wobble his way between walls.
And we thought with agony
Of the other cars that would come
Through the long shadow of that night,
Over the hill to the other side, slushing senselessly,
Leaving imprints of frogs, frog rubbings,
Written there like cave paintings, thin as skin.

Argyll

All down the coast
The air was full of fish and sunset.

By nine the lemon-coloured cottages
Were warm windows glowing over the bays.

Far west the light a rim of blue and white,
Jura and Mull and Scarba all carved from shining.

On the way home we stopped to listen to the dark,
To the sea coming huge over a hundred beaches.

In among trees, in windless stillness,
The bats were flitting, weaving patterns with the air.

That night I did not want the stars to rise at all
I wanted it to be like this and nothing more

Looking west into the sunset
To the very end of the world.

Iona

Is this place really nearer to God?
Is the wall thin between our whispers
And his listening? I only know
The world grows less and less –
Here what matters is conquering the wind,
Coming home dryshod, getting the fire lit.
I am not sure whether there is no time here
Or more time, whether the light is stronger
Or just easier to see. That is why
I keep returning, thirsty, to this place
That is older than my understanding,
Younger than my broken spirit.

The Music

He got his tunes that way;
He heard them,
As though they were edges of wind,
As if he saw the notes
In the loud rattle of the storm,
In the darkness – coming out of nothing.
He listened for them, as though they were bees
In ones and twos to begin with,
Then a swarm, a black net, a mist.
He had to catch them in the bow of his fiddle,
He had to find them before they passed,
Were gone and lost forever.

Where did they come from, those notes?
It was as though they had been sent to find him
Through the rampaging of Atlantic gales,
Or else had blown off course
Like a ship's cargo, like a pirate treasure hold,
Had spilled onto St Kilda, into his hands,
Into the fiddle,
Till it was filled brimful.

He wrote none of them down.
He caught them when they came;
He caught them in the net of his listening,
Recognised and remembered them,
Stored them in his head as the others
Stored fish and birds for winter.

They lay in the dark of his head
Like gold in the depths of a cave.
They died with him too
The day his eyes glazed and their light
Failed and faded for ever. The tunes were blown out
And back into the wind.

Islands

Harris is tweed moorland
A moon-landing in high wind.

Staffa is an organ
Thrown overboard by Mendelssohn.

Skye is hairpin bends
Pen nib hills inking wet cloud.

Jura is a fight with bracken
A Nessie of humps on the far horizon.

Lewis is rusted villages
Lost among sermons and whisky.

Pearls

They were the reason the Romans came here –
River things, spun into milky globes over years and years.
I often wonder who it was who found them first,
Those mussels, dark shells whorled and folded
Like hands in prayer, embedded in feet of shingle.

The travellers knew where they were. The unsettled people
Who followed the seasons, the stars, yearned only the open
                                                    road.
They carried the knowledge of pearls inside them, secret,
Could tell the very bend of river each pearl had come from –
This one like the pale globe of Venus at dawn,
This one a skylark's egg, and this the blush of a young girl's
                                                    lips.

Yet the Romans never reached the Highland rivers
Where the best pearls slept. They were kept out
By the painted people, the Pictish hordes
Bristling on the border like bad weather.

The pearls outlived even the travellers, whose freedom
Was bricked into the big towns long enough ago,
Who did not understand any longer
The language of the land.

In the last part of the north,
In the startling blue of the rivers,
The shells still grow. Their pearls are stories
That take a hundred years to tell.

Rumbling Bridge

One summer afternoon you go
Up the silvering of the river, low
Under the green cathedral of the leaves
Lemoned by sunlight, the slow wheel of gold
High in the huge sky.
Up there, above the flutes of the falls
You lower yourself into the delicious gasp of river
Rock downwards through stone gullies,
Fleeces of water, deep runnels, curls and eddies,
Smoothings the colour of whisky.
You stay water-tobogganing the whole day long until the
                                                    sun

Has bled to death behind the hills,
Till the wind whispers in the trees, shudders them,
And everything is only different shades of blue.
You trail home with sandshoes
As a slip of moon lifts over the pine trees
And the bats weave their own mime through June air.
You come home and stand
And don't want to go inside,
Don't want to close your door on this day
Till the last of the light is lost.

Hebrides

This shattered place, this place of fragments,
A play of wind and sea and light,
Shifting always, becoming and diminishing;
Out of nowhere the full brightness of morning
Blown away, buried and lost.

And yet, it you have faith, if you wait long enough,
There will be the miracle of an otter
Turning water into somersaults;
The jet blackness of a loch brought back to life
By the sudden touch of sun.

But you will take nothing home with you
Save your own changedness,
And this wind that will waken you
Sometimes, all your life, yearning to return.

Galway

and suddenly the light coming in gusts
sweeping out over the sea;
the wild irises with their yellow heads
on silver water, on black water,
the duck rising in stretches, in parallel,
against the limestone shoulders of the hills –
their shale grey strangeness –
before the cloud bruises, the rain scatters
in muslin veils and all is wintered
on this journey, this voyage through moments,
that catch for a second like sunlight
to be beheld and marvelled
before all of it changes and your hands are empty;
only the memory
left as light as the imprint of a leaf
upon your life
for ever.

The Fishing

Five days they'd be away, he said,
Touching soft the gold beneath her neck.

Their boat was gone in a squall of gulls
The water danced with light.

Her three burst in, an overturned bundle
Of half-told tales and tangled clothes.

She hung things on a salt wind
That beat like wings the blue dusk.

A whole moon rolled into that huge sky,
The hills shrank back to dark.

And she lay listening,
October rattling the sleeping house

She lay awake until the light
Bled morning red:

All day and the next day
She did everything and she did nothing.

Shoes

The shoemaker stitched and sewed
In the dark scent of his own world. Once a year
I went in there, to the black adverts for boots and polish
Rusty over the walls of his shop. I blinked

Like something that had tumbled down a hole
Into the heart of the earth. Even the air was tanned,
The chestnut of shoes burnished and perfect from hands
That had poured in the pure oils of their love,

Their labour. He wiped those huge hands on his apron,
Stood as I smoothed my feet into the mended shoes,
Looking, his eyes like a calf's, brown,
In an air that was brown, a brown cave.

The scent of leather hung in the air
In my shoes that were good as new,
That fitted my feet like hooves –
They shone so I saw my own smile.

I went out into the blue breeze of the springtime,
Watching my step, all the way home. Still,
School scuffed them and skinned them,
Reduced them at last to a shadow of all they had been.

The Bat

It smelled of muslin, dank and dark,
This fallen newborn lying in the crystals
Of an early morning dew.

The size of my child's thumb;
Wings in segments that folded in on one another,
Tight bead of eyes.

In it were all the myths and legends
That had flown into the six years
Of my lying awake in the night.

But when I held it I was not afraid;
It was made of such soft intricacy
That I smoothed the fur of its head,

Whispered a prayer
As I slipped into a grave
No larger than a snowdrop.

Awakening

Out of twelve acorns I picked in the wood
Just one grew tall. I'd been away
The first half of July, came back
To thunder, floods, a garden gone to seed.
And then, that evening, I saw the stem
Rising high as my hand.

I bent to behold a miracle, the bitterness
Of weeds and grass all gone.
I touched three leaves – crinkled things
With cut-out edges, like those of grown-up oaks.
Eleven acorns still lay fast asleep
Deep in dark earth. One had become a tree.

Sometimes

There are nights we hang out the washing –
Autumn nights, when the copper-coloured land
Whispers dry with fire and wind.

We drag out the sheets at midnight
Like the sails of great white ships
Haul them over the lines to bloom and blow.

A huge moon wobbles from behind the hills
Silvers into the sky and shines
So we blink and have to shield our eyes.

Wind and moonlight, gusts of wind and moonlight;
The world is made of wind and moonlight,
And the sheets creak and breathe the whole night long.

The Heron

The heron is a Presbyterian minister
Standing gloomy in his long grey coat
Looking at his own reflection in a Sabbath loch.

Every now and again, pronouncing fire and brimstone,
He snatches at an unsuspecting trout
And stands with a lump in his throat.

The congregation of midges laughs at him in Gaelic;
He only prays for them, head bent into grey rain,
As a lark sings psalms half a mile above.

Midnight Sun

The boat furled out in a pale hum
Over water clear as glass
A whole half hour. Then the engine melted.

Nothing. Just the mountains inland
Torched by sunlight, just five gulls
Dipping near us, leaving pearls.

We pulled twenty fish from the heavy timelessness of that
water,
Dragged them flapping, gaping for air,
Into the huge blue light of July.

Over them the water shut once more
Like the biggest door in the world. We turned at last,
Ploughed home through blood and salt.

Meeting

Today I met a journeyman thatcher.
He had not been born with that life in his blood;
One day he just dug up his roots and left,
Never looked back.

He said that sometimes as he swept the thatch
Up onto a roof and heard the shingle of the trees,
The fields' chase, he was blown
Out of the mad motorway of this age

To a place that you never could buy,
A place that is on no map.
He had heard it and touched it in roofs,
In thatch, just once or twice, for a moment.

In him now the back lanes, the side roads
Of a timeless time, a land where hay ricks
Still jolt and topple. I sensed the sunlight in him
Warm as a whole summer.

Swallows

One day when spring has come again to green the trees
And in the fields the flowers bend and blow
The swallows swim the air, they play the breeze,
Returned three thousand miles across the flow
And swell of tides, the moiling of the seas.
And no-one's ever found, and no-one knows,
What strength it is that brings them back to free
Their flight above our lives, our serried rows
Of terraced worlds and ordered days of ease.
Yet now the west winds change, the old earth tilts
A fraction in her chains, the light goes grey
So through the wood a chase of bright leaves spins.
The dark begins to grow, the autumn wilts
And every dusk the swallows flit and play,
Their sojourn all but done, their time here in.
We stare at winter windows all day long
Watching where they were, knowing they are gone.

A Little Miracle

Two black and brown puffs of duckling,
Little bits of thistledown,
That could have blown away in a breeze –
Bobbing beneath the bank of the river.

As I approached they shot out into the current,
Were washed away like flotsam,
Making high peeps of sound
Till a bend snatched them from sight.

All night I worried for them,
Went out into the raining darkness,
To the lion roar of the river,
Listened in hope for their peeping.

And I wondered that such little things survived at all,
Winter and spring, the angry traffic of this world,
To grow safe and strong into wings –
To learn to fly.

September

The fields lay white beneath a snow of sun
And birds were restless underneath, they rose and wheeled
Like silver leaves. The skies were more than blue;
Burnished and beaten with a strange brilliance.
The angels are coming, I thought;
The angels will come in the night
When a huge moon ovals through these bright and cloudless
                                                    skies;
They will come to bind the sheaves
While we are fast asleep.
They will work the fields, their wings tight-folded,
All through the white night of this September,
The moon gliding high like a balloon
Over the glazed harvest of the world;
Nothing moving except the angels and the wind, until the
                                                    task is done
In the warm stillness of the dawn.

Mushrooms

The night before a great moon full of honey
Had flowed up behind the hills and poured across the fields

The leaves were rusting, the wheat whispered
Dry and gold in the wind's hands.

Andrew and I went to Foss. We drove over the hills
That were blustery with huge gusts of sunlight.

We stopped and walked to the loch, left two trails
Through the grass, came on the mushrooms by accident,

A village of strewn white hats
The folds of their gills underneath as soft as skin.

We almost did not want to take them, as if
It would be theft – wronging the hills, the trees, the grass.

But in the end we did, we picked them with reverence,
And they broke like bread between our hands, we carried
them home

Pieces of field, smelling of earth and autumn;
A thanksgiving, a blessing.

The Wind and the Moon

The wind woke me, the loud howl of it
Boomed round the house and I felt at sea;
I fastened my eyes and was out in a ship,
Ten miles of Atlantic. I went to the window,
Watched the whole round of the moon
Ploughing through clouds, a coin
Of silver and gold.

All night I was blown between dreams,
Never slept deep, was thinking
Of the trees crashing and rising with wind,
Of the chestnut rain that would fall
By the morning.

At dawn I woke up, went out
Into the bright blue whirl of the wind,
Rode the wild horse of it upwards
Into the wood and beyond,
To the hill with the chestnut trees,
The leaves dancing at my feet
Russet and gold.

I ran and ran till my chest
Hurt with my heart. Under the hands of the chestnuts
That waved and swung in the air,
Saddles of leather, polished and shining,
Broken from the beds of their shells –
A whole hoard.

I went home in a gust of light
My pockets and hands
Knobbled with conkers.

The Novemberland

Something wonderful there is in coming home
A ragged, late November night,

Leaving town and entering a midnight black,
Rain splintering the glass.

Headlights dig from darkness two white beams,
Rendering the other outer world so huge,

The car panthering the lanes,
Tunnelling a dusk that's roofed with branches.

Furry paws of wind come and nudge the car,
The trees above all wave like soundless cries.

And then an owl, a padded softness of a thing,
Suddens the eyes, glides through light and vanishes.

Until a long hour afterwards, at last,
Home's amber cave floods whole the heart,

Tyres crackle gravel and the engine shudders still,
A crystalling of stars engulfs the sky –

And silence pours back in to fill the night.

The Stars

From the age of five my sight was smudged as a mole's;
I wore tortoishell-rimmed glasses that were never quite
                                                    clean
And the stars looked white and indistinct
Vague pearls in a distant heaven.
On my fifteenth birthday my parents gave me lenses –
Little cupped things that drifted into sight across my irises.
Driving home with them that night I suddenly caught sight
                                                    of something,
Got out by the edge of the field and looked,
Amazed and disbelieving as if Christ himself had healed my
                                                    eyes,
For the stars were crackling and sparking
Like new-cut diamonds on the velvet of a jeweller's
                                                    window,
So near and clear I could have stretched and held them
Carried them home in my own pocket.
That was the gift my parents gave me on my birthday –
The stars.

A Poem For Ann

Three feet small
With dreams as big as Christmas.

A cornfield of curls
And a smile that would melt a soldier.

When you cry
All of you falls to pieces;
Everyone comes running to mend you.

At night your eyes look huge;
You are afraid of the owl
That ghosts your bedroom window.

I tell you a story
But you are kingdoms and princes away
Long before the ending.

In the morning I will bring you blackbirds
And put the sun on your pillow.
I will tie your laces,
And pray safe roads for your feet.

Jura

From Carsaig you can see it,
Three peaks rising up out of the Atlantic,
Like a sea monster, the ridge of a dragon's back.
What is there to find but a scattering of houses,
A road, a hotel, then nothing.
It drifts into mist, a huge loneliness,
Composed of bracken and moor and cave.
Who comes to look? Who bothers
To cross the few sea miles
To watch some great mound of empty stone
Drift into the distance?
This busy world would think it worthless –
A barren landfall on the edge of sanity.
To me it is wondrous that such things should still remain,
Uncharted and untamed, like eagles.

The Deer

Come December they click at nightfall,
When the hills are ghostly with snow,
Flint-hoofed into a town iced by moonlight.

They are whittled from wood;
Sinews of strength sewn together,
Their hearing honed to catch the slightest falls in the forest
Or know the click of a gun.

Their mouths soften the grass of gardens
Before dogs nose them, bound out barking, big-voiced,
Send them no louder than a scattering of leaves
Back into the huge night.

Once Before

About Christmas-time we could go there,
By the back roads, with fields of geese and a grey snow.
It was flat land, tousled in autumn with red clusters
And long stretches of poplar. The old couple
Were hewn from ash and the blown-down tree of a lost age
They sat behind windows of blue-cold cloud,
Welcomed us with fire and tea, green rooms of holly.
And he would take goose quills in his frayed grasp,
Skill ink pens with a knife and tut his pipe.
There would be talk and a looking at old things;
The clock in the hall and the skates with their many
                                                  winters,
Curled asleep in a box. Then the dark came
With frost of rough gemstones, the air pinched
With stars and balloons of breath. We had to go
That year and the year that came after,
And now I don't know the way back.

The Slide

We longed for the sharp crinkle of December stars,
That ghostly mist like cobwebs in the grass –
Ten degrees below zero.

After the snow came petalling from the skies,
Settled into a deep quilt, the frost
Diamonded the top, making a thick crust.

On the long descent of the lawn
We made our slide, planed the ground
Hour after hour till it smiled with ice.

At night we teetered out with buckets,
Rushed the water down the slide's length
In one black stain.

Next day the slide was lethal,
A curling glacier that shot us downhill
In a single hiss.

Even after the thaw greened our world again
The slide remained written in the grass
As long as our stories.

The Winter Bridge

Dead winter. Fifteen geese
Went north in the shape of horns.

The river had stopped talking,
Clenched hard as a dead man's fist.

Bronze swords of sun battled the ridges,
Legends went by like horses in the mist.

At four the light melted into gold
And a wedding ring of moon
Slipped onto a branch of birch.

This Year

not before January the snow
a day thin blue as a bird's shell

the skies grazed with storm
a great grey closing over the sea

not more than flickers of skin
thin on the wind

then flocking the air, lashes of cotton
pattering and soft

settling over us, a blanket of silence
filling the trees with shapes

when night cleared in a clustering of stars
the roads deep and the power gone

I realised we had not come far at all

Trust

Five days the snow had lain
Deep as a boot. Mouths of ice
Hung from roofs and windows,
The river slid by like a wolf.

At noon I went out with crumbs
Cupped in one hand. As I crouched,
A robin fluttered from nowhere,
Grasped the landfall of my palm.

A rowan eye inspected me
Side on. The blood-red throat
Swelled and sank, breathing quickly,
Till hungry, the beak stabbed fast.

The robin finished, turned,
Let out one jewel of sound,
Then ruffled up into the sky –
A skate on the frosty air.

Remember

There will be only a few days like this –
The low sun flinting the house
Through the green sea of the trees as you stand
Struck, blessed, bathed in the same light
That rose life once from the young earth, that appled
The first child's cheeks.
There will be only a few days like this
To stop doing and stand, blinking,
As the leverets tumble in the bright field
And a cuckoo's moss voice calls from a far wood.
Wait until the sun has gone in broken orange
Down beneath the hills, and the blue sky
Hurts with the sudden shudder of the dusk.
Give thanks and turn and go back home
For there will be only a few days like this.